GOOD HOUSEKEEPING
PATCHWORK
AND
APPLIQUÉ

GOOD HOUSEKEEPING
PATCHWORK
AND
APPLIQUÉ

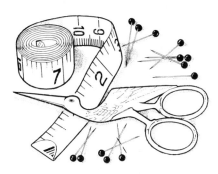

EBURY PRESS

Chief Contributor/Art Editor
Michele Walker

Editor
Miren Lopategui

Assistant Editor
Maria Mosby

Managing Editor
Amy Carroll

Managing Art Editor
Debbie Mackinnon

Good Housekeeping Patchwork and Appliqué
was conceived, edited and designed by
Dorling Kindersley Limited, 9 Henrietta Street, London WC2E 8PS

First published in Great Britain in 1981 by
Ebury Press, National Magazine House,
72 Broadwick Street, London W1V 2BP
Second impression 1982

ISBN 0 85223 203 9

Printed and bound in Italy by Arnoldo Mondadori, Verona

Contents

✤

✤

Introduction

Increased leisure time in recent years has led to a revival of interest in handicrafts, and patchwork and appliqué are no exception. Apart from being economical they are easy to work and, most important of all, provide limitless scope for individual experimentation with colour, patterns and texture while at the same time making attractive and colourful things for the home and wardrobe.

The origins of both crafts date back to times of antiquity, with earliest records showing their use in Ancient Egypt as far back as 1000 BC. Although developed and used for hundreds of years in North Africa and the Middle and Far East, it was not until the eleventh century that they were introduced into Europe by the Crusaders returning from Palestine, where their use in richly-decorated flags, banners and wall-hangings had been much admired.

Despite their continued use in Europe, however, it was the eighteenth- and nineteenth-century North American settlers who were responsible for the flourishing of both patchwork and appliqué. Originally they used the techniques for purely economic and utilitarian reasons: scraps of fabric were pieced to make warm bedcovers and quilts, and also to patch up holed and worn-away fabrics. Making patchworks and exchanging patterns and ideas created ideal opportunities for social gatherings – quilting bees – which provided entertainment during the lonely winter months. Block patterns were developed, and given names such as *Log cabin* and *Birds in the air*, which reflected the simple lifestyle of the early pioneers.

Distinctive styles of patchwork emerged, from the plain, geometric bold-coloured patterns of the Mennonite and Amish quilts, to the spontaneous, free appliqué Pennsylvania Dutch designs, and patchwork came to be regarded as a very important form of American folk art.

While patchwork and appliqué are still excellent ways of using up scraps of fabric and are, thus, still very economical crafts, they have, over the years, also evolved into new and exciting art forms. This book deals with the complete range of patchwork designs, from the simple one-patch to the more intricate pieced block, framed or medallion, crazy, appliqué and dyed and sprayed patterns. The vast range of modern fabrics and dyes, together with the endless possibilities for colour combinations and interpretation of patterns, offers the contemporary patchworker an opportunity to create exciting and original designs using only the simplest sewing materials found in every home.

BASIC TECHNIQUES

Fabric samples

EQUIPMENT

Both patchwork and appliqué require accurate craftsmanship, and it is worthwhile investing in some good basic equipment.

For designing and making templates

Metal ruler; 2H pencil; coloured pencils; glue; graph paper (square and isometric); scissors (for paper templates); knife; mounting card; tracing paper; notepaper; set square; protractor; pair of compasses.

For sewing the patchwork

Sewing threads and beeswax; needles; thimble; lace pins; scissors (for fabric); seam ripper; iron and pressing cloth; sewing machine (optional); tape measure.

FABRIC

For hand sewing, and particularly for patterns using diamonds and small patches, closely-woven cottons are easiest to handle and give the best results. Heavier fabrics, such as tweeds and corduroys, are suitable for larger pieces and machine sewing. It is not advisable to combine light and heavy fabrics within the same piece as the heavy ones will pull the lighter fabrics out of shape. By using iron-on interfacing, however, a lighter fabric can be given extra weight. Before use all fabrics should be washed, to test for colour fastness and shrinkage, and then ironed.

The most difficult fabrics to handle are synthetics and any which are stretchy, loosely-woven or crease-resistant.

Choose patterned material carefully. Large prints can overdominate while small ones tend to merge into each other unless contrasted with plain fabrics.

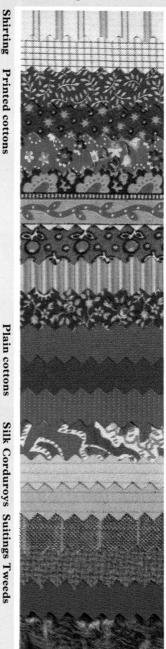

Shirting   Printed cottons   Plain cottons   Silk   Corduroys   Suitings   Tweeds

7

Patchwork

Before a patchwork pattern is chosen, you should first decide what you want to make, its size and whether you want to sew it by hand or machine. There are three methods of sewing patchwork: first by machine, which gives the strongest results and is particularly good for heavier fabrics; second by hand, using a small running stitch – this is how most traditional American patchworks were made – and, thirdly, by hand, using paper templates. This last method, which takes the longest time, gives very accurate results and is usually associated with traditional English patchwork.

SIZE

For a beginner, smaller items such as cushions, cot quilts or wall-hangings, are good projects to try. They will enable you to become familiar with patchwork techniques without being overwhelmed by size. When making a cushion cover, buy the pad first and make the cover 25mm (1in) smaller – a patchwork cushion cover looks best when it is a tight fit. To estimate the size of a patchwork bedcover, drape a sheet over the bed and take the measurements from it. In this way you will be able to estimate the size required to cover the pillows and blankets, and to calculate the overhang.

CHOOSING A PATTERN

Once you have decided on the project and its size you can then start choosing a pattern. Pick one that both interests you and fits your purpose. Try and relate it to the size of the finished piece – it is important that the individual pieces should not be too small and difficult to sew, or so large that they look clumsy and out of scale on the finished project. Patterns that have large repeats, such as *Irish chain*, which is made from two separate blocks, are not suitable for small projects. Crazy patchwork, on the other hand, has a random pattern and can be easily shaped for many purposes including clothes.

The amount of time you have available is also an important consideration: some patterns, such as *Tumbling blocks* and *Grandmother's flower garden*, are best made by hand using papers, and take much longer than, say, *Log cabin*, which can be made quickly with a machine.

Medallion patterns, basically a central design surrounded by a number of borders, need to be planned carefully beforehand. The borders must relate to each other in both size and colour.

DESIGN

Before sewing, work out size, pattern colours and textures. If the design is based on a repeated block, trace off any pattern from this book and colour it in. Try several colour variations, then put four blocks together – straight block-to-block setting gives the most potential for pattern-making. As you become more familiar with traditional quilt patterns you will see that most blocks fit into a grid (the number of squares into which a block can be divided). Four-, five-, seven- and nine-patch are the most common. This grid system will give a good idea of how the block is put together.

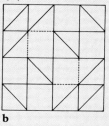

a *Four* Double X *blocks give a pattern not apparent from looking at a single block.*

b *A 4-patch pattern can be divided into 4 squares, or multiples of 4.*

a   **b**

While it is important for the scale of the block to suit the size of project, when using traditional patterns it is not always possible to work to a set size because block patterns tend to be squares of 20–30cm (8–12in). Generally, a pattern made from a number of smaller blocks is more interesting than one which uses only a few over-sized blocks. To increase the area of patchwork, without making extra blocks, alternate the pieced blocks with squares of printed or plain fabric. The size can also be increased by setting the blocks with lattice strips which also act as good harmonizers of colours in a scrap quilt. Borders are also useful because they help make the patchwork fit a required size and also frame the work.

One-patch patterns do not have as many variations as block designs but it is still important to plan first. It is a good idea to divide the fabrics first into colour categories, before assembling the patches. Then make the final arrangement before sewing.

Finally, it is important to make a scale drawing. This will show the relative size of the patterns and is useful for determining borders. You can easily estimate how many templates are needed and the number of patches from each colour. This drawing is an invaluable guide for making up the patchwork.

TEMPLATES

Once the design has been chosen, the templates can be made. These must be accurate because they are the patterns from which each shape is cut out in a given design. An error in size, however slight, will compound to several centimetres over an entire piece of work.

Templates should always be cut from a strong material that will keep its shape, such as mounting card. Medium-weight sandpaper is also ideal and it has the added advantage of adhering to the fabric. Many of the geometric shapes used in patchwork can be drawn from graph paper, then cut out and stuck on mounting card or sandpaper.

Cutting templates from square and isometric paper

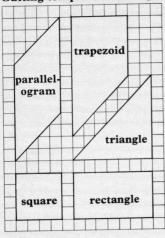

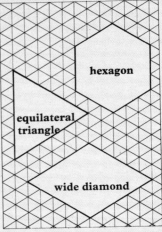

There are two diamond shapes which are commonly used in patchwork: the 60°–120° diamond, used for six-pointed stars, hexagons and *Tumbling blocks* (this can be cut from the triangular grid graph paper); and the long 45°–135° diamond, which has to be drawn with a set square and a pair of compasses.

Constructing the long diamond

Draw AB. Using a protractor or set square draw AC at 45° from AB making it the same length as AB. With the compass point on C, make an arc. With the point on B, make another arc to cut the first one at D. Join BD and CD.

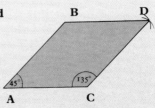

Templates for machine sewing

The size of these includes the finished size of the patch plus a seam allowance of 6mm ($\frac{1}{4}$in) or 9mm ($\frac{3}{8}$in). Whatever size seam allowance is chosen, it must remain consistent throughout.

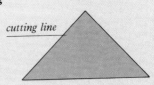

cutting line

Templates for hand sewing without papers

These are window templates (empty frames). The inner edge represents finished size of the patch and is the sewing line. The outer edge is fabric cutting line. Give these templates a firmer marking edge by making seam allowance 9mm ($\frac{3}{8}$in).

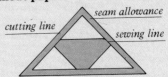

seam allowance
cutting line
sewing line

To keep the window template rigid, leave the central area uncut.

Templates for hand sewing with papers

Three templates are needed: one made 6mm ($\frac{1}{4}$in) bigger on all sides (used for cutting the fabric); the second made to the exact size of the finished patch (used for backing papers), and the third is a window template for patterned fabrics, the same size as the first template (used for framing the printed fabric).

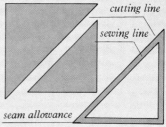

ESTIMATING THE FABRIC

Unless you are making a patchwork from scraps it is important to estimate accurately the amount of fabric needed. This can only be done when all templates are cut and the number of pieces is known.

Always include seam allowances when estimating fabric. The width of fabric is usually 90cm (36in) or 115cm (45in). See how many times the template can be laid across the width. For example, if using fabric 90cm (36in) wide, and a template 8cm ($3\frac{1}{4}$in) square you will get eleven squares to a width. To estimate the length of fabric needed, divide the number of squares required by the number of times a template fits across the width of fabric and multiply the result by the width of the template. So, if you need one hundred squares, calculate thus: $100 \div 11 \times 8\text{cm}$ ($3\frac{1}{4}$in) = 72cm (29in). It is advisable to add a little extra so, in this case, 90cm (36in) of fabric would be adequate. Borders and lattice strips are estimated in the same way, using the width of the fabric as a basis of measurement.

MARKING AND CUTTING THE FABRIC

Fabric for patchwork is always marked on the wrong side with a well-sharpened pencil. It is a good idea to use a dark-coloured pencil for light fabrics and a light colour for dark fabrics.

When placing the template on the fabric, align the sides with the straight- or cross-grain where possible, avoiding the bias of the fabric, which has most stretch. Fit the templates flush together.

Some patchwork shapes, such as the trapezoid, have definite right and wrong sides and are not reversible like the square or the rectangle. When cutting these non-reversible shapes, place the template wrong side up on the wrong side of the fabric.

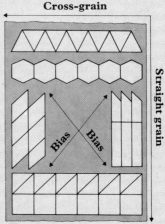

The selvedge edges run parallel to the straight grain which has minimum stretch.

SEWING

When you are ready to start sewing, lay out all the patchwork shapes in the correct order so that you can check the pattern for any mistakes and view the design as a whole. Not all hand sewing can be done by machine so it is useful to know both techniques, but two principles apply to both. First, use straight seams and avoid sewing into corners. Second, it is much easier to join the smallest pieces into progressively bigger units until the patchwork is complete. The technique is illustrated below, in this case for the *Sherman's march* block.

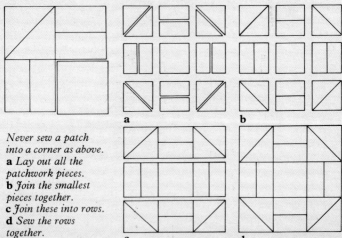

Never sew a patch into a corner as above.
a *Lay out all the patchwork pieces.*
b *Join the smallest pieces together.*
c *Join these into rows.*
d *Sew the rows together.*

Machine sewing

This is the quickest method of making patchwork and is suitable for all shapes that are not too small (less than 4cm [1½in]). Set the machine to about five stitches per centimetre (twelve per inch). Choose a needle size suitable for the fabric being sewn and use cotton polyester thread. The patches must be accurately cut because in machine sewing the edge of the fabric is aligned against the edge of the presser foot which usually determines a seam allowance of 6mm (¼in). On some machines it may be easier to align the fabric with the seam allowance incised on the plate below the foot. If your machine does not have an indicator use masking tape.

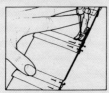
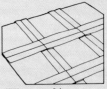

Align edge of fabric with presser foot. Start and end with a back stitch; remove pins before sewing.

Press seams open. When sewing matching seams together, pin either side of seam.

When machine patchwork is complete press all seams open. First press on back and then front.

Hand sewing without papers

Use No. 8 Sharp needles and, if possible, quilting thread which is the strongest. If this is not available, use a waxed cotton-covered polyester. Strands should be no longer than 40cm (16in) and remember to knot the end you cut to prevent twisting. Always mark hand sewn patches on the wrong side of the fabric and never sew through the seam allowance.

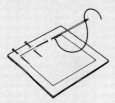

With patches right sides facing pin and match pencil lines. Sew with running stitch, ending with a back stitch.

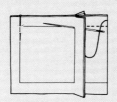

Join rows of patches by first pinning them at corresponding seams. Next sew along matching pencil lines.

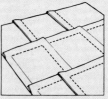

To strengthen seams press to one side – usually the darkest side – or, to avoid lumpiness, alternate the direction.

Hand sewing with papers

This method gives very accurate results and is used for patterns which mainly contain geometric shapes such as hexagons and diamonds although it works equally well with a block design. The fabric is tacked over the paper templates, then the individual patches are overstitched together into rows and the rows formed into larger units. The papers are removed when the patchwork is complete.

Lay patch right side down and pin a paper template to centre. Fold fabric edge over and secure with tape.

Tack all round the patch and carefully remove the masking tape.

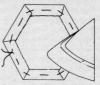

Press the fabric folds – this makes sewing the patches much easier.

Individual patches are first joined with tiny overcasting stitches.

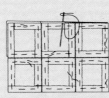

Next the patches are joined into rows, with overcasting stitches.

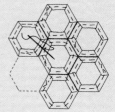

Hexagons can either be joined in rows or formed into rosettes.

BORDERS

Before a border is added, the patchwork should be pressed. Use a cloth to prevent glazing and iron on the back and then the top. Borders can be plain or they can be a contrasting pattern to the patchwork. They are either used as a frame or they can be used to increase a patchwork's size. Either way, they should be planned as part of the patchwork as a whole. The seams should correspond with the seaming of the patchwork and the dimensions must correspond accurately. See below for three different methods for joining borders.

Four-patch border

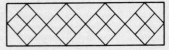

Navajo border

Arrow border

Zigzag border

Straight cut	**Mitred**	**Separate corners**
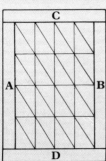	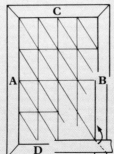	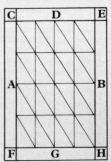
Add A and B (they are same length as patchwork). Now add C and D (width of patchwork plus A and B).	*Cut A and B, also C and D to required size. Fold back diagonally at each corner as shown.*	*Cut A and B to required size. Join C, D, E and F, G, H into 2 separate strips. Join to patchwork.*

EDGING AND LINING

Large patchworks, when finished, need to be lined both to neaten and to strengthen them – and dress-weight cotton is best for this purpose. There are two ways of applying a backing fabric. The first is to cut it the same size as the patchwork and make a separate binding for the edge. The binding can be sewn on in the same order as the straight-cut border, then folded over to the back and hand stitched into position. The second method is to cut the backing fabric 25mm (1in) larger than the top on all sides and bring it over to the front of the patchwork to make a self-binding.

QUILTING

When quilting a patchwork, the edges must be left unfinished until the quilting is completed. For the filling use a synthetic wadding. Mark your quilting pattern on to the patchwork with a coloured pencil. Cut the wadding and backing fabric slightly larger than the patchwork, and tack the three layers together.

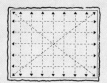

Tack the three layers of fabric together.

Hand quilting

It is advisable to quilt with a frame or hoop. This will keep the three layers of fabric taut and evenly stretched, and will give a puffed effect to the finished quilting. Use a quilting needle and waxed quilting thread; keep the length of thread fairly short and knot the end. Pull the knot through the backing fabric to the wadding. Then, starting in the centre of the design and working outwards, follow the quilting pattern using small, evenly spaced running stitches. Finish off with a couple of back stitches.

The thimble underneath provides a ridge which makes it easier to push the needle through the layers of fabric.

Machine quilting

Machine-quilting is quicker to work than hand-quilting, and gives quite a different effect. It is easier to work if the wadding is not too thick. Use a cotton polyester thread and set the machine to a stitch length suitable to the fabric being used. Quilt the design from the centre outwards and always stitch the quilting lines in opposite directions to prevent the layers from slipping.

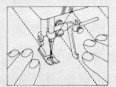

Use your quilting foot attachment so that the fabric does not have to be marked.

TUFTING

If larger patchworks are not quilted the backing and wadding tends to wrinkle and drop. Tufting or tying with a heavy crochet cotton is a quick and effective way of keeping the three layers together. Do not use a synthetic thread because it will not hold in a knot.

Make one stitch through layers, leaving a looped end. Make a back stitch bringing needle out on same side.

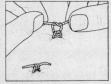

Tie ends of thread with a reef knot. Cut to desired length. Ends can be left on top or underneath.

Finished tufting

Appliqué

Meaning to apply one fabric to another, appliqué can be used for figurative and representational work. Shapes and patterns can be drawn directly onto fabric or cut freely with scissors as in *Flower basket* (p.68). This approach, much freer than patchwork, offers spontaneity of design, and it is a craft that children can tackle with satisfaction. Symmetrical designs can also be made using the folded paper technique as in Hawaiian appliqué (p.71). Appliqué work can be incorporated attractively in a great number of household items, clothes and decorations.

DESIGN

A variety of sources, including paintings and photographs, contain interesting images which can be easily translated into appliqué. Whatever your inspiration, however, aim for bold, simple shapes. Make a draft pattern which will show the different motifs, colours and textures which you plan to incorporate. If the original drawing is too small, it can be enlarged. Trace it and superimpose the tracing paper on graph paper. This will give you a squared drawing that can be scaled up to the required size.

The original design on a square grid.   *Enlarging a detail of the design.*

TEMPLATES

Transfer the draft pattern onto brown paper. Each shape can then be cut out and numbered for identification (it is a good idea to put these numbers also on your original draft pattern). If a shape is to be used several times, it is best to give it added strength by gluing it onto card and then cutting this out.

MARKING AND CUTTING FABRIC

The fabric is marked on the right side. For the appliqué to lie flat, the straight grain of the appliqué shape should run the same way as the straight of the fabric to which it is applied.

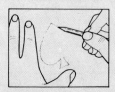  

Mark around the edge of the design with a well-sharpened, appropriately-coloured pencil.   *Cut all the fabric pieces 6mm ($\frac{1}{4}$in) larger than the finished marked shape.*   *Clip curved edges of fabric pieces close to pencil line; this helps when folding seam.*

SEWING

There are several ways of sewing appliqué but, whichever method is used, the work must remain neat with smooth, flat edges and no fraying. Not all edges need to be turned under: when possible tuck the raw edge under a hemmed edge of an adjacent piece. When pinning the final arrangement of pieces in place, position the large background shapes first and then build up to the front shapes. Tack all pieces into position.

Tack about 3mm (⅛in) from the folded edge before sewing.

Hand sewing

Use a No. 8 Sharp needle and, if possible, quilting thread. If this is unavailable, use wax cotton-covered polyester thread. Its colour should match the appliqué, not the ground fabric. Use blind, running or overcast stitch to attach appliqué to the fabric.

Blind stitch	Overcast stitch	Running stitch

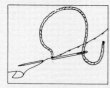 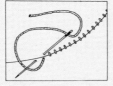 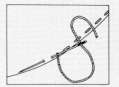

A hidden stitch where the needle is worked through seam fold of appliqué to ground fabric.

Pass needle through back of fabric and into appliqué to make a small, diagonal stitch.

Insert needle from back of work, taking several stitches onto it before pulling it through.

Machine sewing

A method which is particularly suited to making clothes, machine sewing is quicker and stronger than hand sewing but not necessarily easier and the stitches cannot be hidden. Prepare the appliqué pieces as for hand sewing and tack to the foundation. Use a straight, zigzag or satin stitch. If the latter is used the edges can be left raw. Do not use a back stitch to begin and end, take threads to the back instead.

FINISHING

When all the sewing is complete, remove the tacking and press on the right side with a cloth. To prevent a dark ground fabric from showing through, cut the ground fabric up to 6mm (¼in) from the stitching line. This also helps keep the work flat.

Carefully remove ground fabric to reduce thickness.

For adding borders and quilting see Patchwork pp.14-15

ONE PATCH

Some of the most traditional patterns –
particularly those of English design – are created from
single-shape geometric patches. These patches are all the
same size and, when repeated, give an overall mosaic effect.
One-patch patterns, because of their simplicity of design,
depend upon skilful use of colour to create an impact.
This type of patchwork is traditionally sewn by hand
using backing papers.

Trip around the world

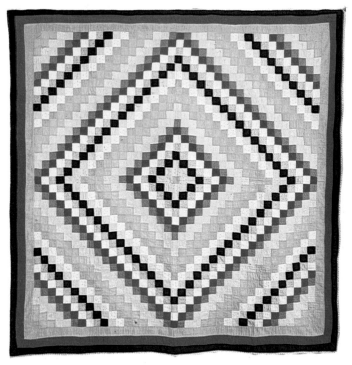

Pennsylvanian quilt 1880-90 The bright colours of this quilt are typical of those used by the early German settlers who tended to use plain rather than printed fabrics. This pattern is composed of squares sewn together to create an expanding diamond design.

Materials The success of the design depends on choosing bright colours in tones ranging from light to dark. Cotton fabrics, either plain or with small prints, are the most suitable and offer the widest colour range. Shirting material is also useful for the lighter tones.

Uses An excellent beginner's pattern, it is really best suited to a large square quilt. Unless the squares are very small it is difficult to show enough colour contrast on a small quilt or cushion. On a child's quilt, colour gradation will be more effective with a diagonal pattern.

Construction *Trip around the world* can quickly and easily be made on a machine. Finished squares of about 50–65mm (2–2½in) make a reasonable-size quilt and are not too difficult to handle. Mark out the pattern on graph paper first and then use this as a guide for cutting and sewing the pieces together. To achieve a central square there must be an uneven number of squares and rows. The squares are joined to make rows and then the rows are joined into a single piece. Begin piecing in the top left corner, working left to right, using the pattern as a guide. Remember to pin either side of seams for alignment and press flat with an iron. Add several plain strips for the border.

Pyramids

American quilt 1910 A simple pattern made from light and dark triangles that presents a continual illusion of larger shapes.

Materials A wide variety of light and dark closely-woven fabrics.
Uses The optical illusion, which gives this pattern added interest, is only visible on a large project such as a quilt or wall-hanging.

Construction This pattern, alternating strips of light and dark triangles, can be sewn by hand or machine. The strips are sewn into rows, again the lights and darks are alternated, and the points of each shape carefully matched. The illusion of larger triangles is created when three darker shapes are pieced together. Add a separate binding or a wider border to frame the design.

Repeat pattern

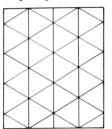

Sew in vertical rows adding a half triangle at each end before sewing the rows together.

Strip quilt

A contemporary quilt made from strips of heavy-weight fabrics, chosen for their textures and warmth of colour.

Materials Any fabrics of similar weight can be used. Heavier materials are better for larger projects; ribbons and lace are more suitable for smaller items.
Uses The strip technique can be used for quilts, cushions or clothes.

Construction Use a machine for heavy fabrics. Cut the fabric into equal-length strips. On the wrong side of the backing fabric, mark the centre vertical and horizontal lines. Start in the centre and lay one strip across the backing fabric, pin. Tuck the next strip under the first one, pin. Stitch along the bottom edge of the first strip, leaving a seam allowance and securing both strips onto the base fabric. Continue in this way until the first half of the patchwork is completed. Return to the centre and complete the second half. When the top is finished fringe the raw edges of the strips. Bind edges.

Tumbling blocks

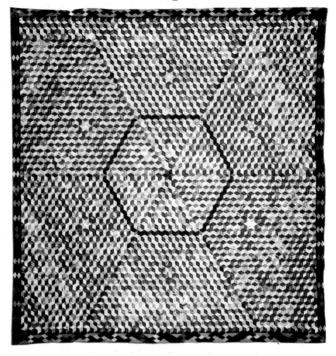

Mid-nineteenth-century English coverlet A typical example of work produced by the "gentlewomen" of that period. The signatures on this one suggest it was made by two sisters. These patchworks were rarely quilted and were made for decoration rather than warmth. The elaborate one-patch designs used a variety of silks, ribbons and brocades and displayed superb workmanship.

Materials To retain the fine points of the diamond shape, closely-woven cottons and silks are best. To create a three-dimensional effect, definite light, medium and dark shades are needed.
Uses Tumbling blocks work equally well on smaller projects such as a cushion. This type of patchwork is most successful made by hand using paper templates so the size of the finished work depends on how much time and patience are available!

Construction Use a 60°–120° wide diamond template. The backing papers must be accurate for the pieces to fit together and for the finished patchwork to lie flat. Tumbling blocks are usually made up with one dark, one medium and one light-coloured patch. On this patchwork the colour sequence is changed to make dark steps for the hexagon outline, light stars in each of the sections and a dark star in the centre. Make up this pattern in rows rather than individual blocks.

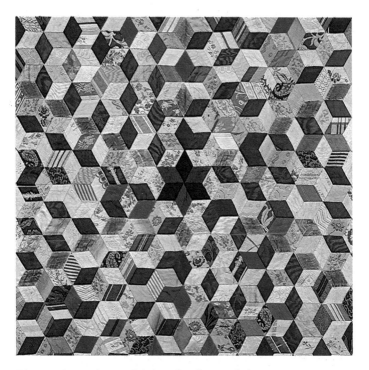

Diamond template

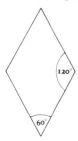

Cut a wide diamond from isometric graph paper.

Joining the diamonds into rows

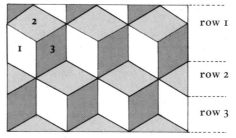

row 1

row 2

row 3

Join a light (1), medium (2) and dark (3) patch together. Continue to make the first row in this way. Then add the second row of medium patches, followed by the third row of alternating light and dark patches. Continue in this way until the patchwork is completed.

Finishing The edges of the patchwork can be turned under or quarter- and half-shape diamonds can be made to fill the edges and corners.

Sunburst

Mennonite quilt 1880 The Mennonites are a religious sect living in Pennsylvania. Their sophisticated handling of patterns and colours makes their work quite distinctive. The eight-pointed star of this design is made entirely of diamond shapes.

Materials This quilt is made from woollen fabrics, but closely-woven cottons are easier to fold around the points of each diamond. Planning is essential for this pattern in order to relate light and dark tones and give a radiating effect of colour.

Uses This star can be used to create an overall repeated pattern or a single dramatic image. *Sunburst* is not a beginner's pattern.

Construction The template is a long diamond (45°–135°) which requires very accurate cutting and sewing. It can be made by any of the three construction methods described on pages 12–13. Using papers guarantees accuracy but, for a large project, machine sewing is much quicker. Each segment of the large star is made up of sixty-four diamonds. The segments are made up individually then joined together. The eight points must meet and fit accurately in the centre so that the patchwork will lie flat.

| **Template** | **One segment** | **Joining the star** |

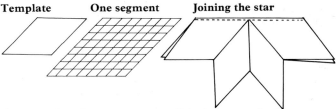

Construct a long diamond (see p. 10).
Each segment has eight rows of
eight diamonds.

Join the star together in separate
halves each made up from 4
segments. Join along centre seam.

Finishing To make up the star
into a square add a square to
each corner and a right-angle
triangle between each of the
centre points. Alternatively, the
star can be appliquéd onto a
background fabric.

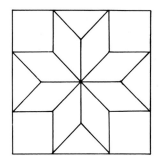

Grandmother's flower garden

English patchwork 1850-60 One of a pair of quilts almost identical in design. Each one contains over 6,000 pieces all neatly assembled with the backing papers still intact.

Materials This is a scrap-bag patchwork that successfully uses a great variety of printed fabrics. Generally, hexagon patterns are best made from cotton fabrics of even weights because these can be folded more neatly over the backing papers.
Uses The hexagon, which is always associated with traditional English patchwork, is suitable for small or large projects. The patches can be sewn together in a random pattern or grouped to form individual rosettes.

Construction The best way of making a hexagon pattern is to hand sew it using backing papers. *Grandmother's flower garden* is usually made up of one centre hexagon, surrounded by a circle of six hexagons in a second colour, surrounded by a circle of twelve hexagons in a third colour. Large hexagons can be joined by machine using a zig-zag stitch but this method is not suitable for small, difficult-to-handle patches.

Sewing sequence

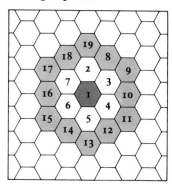

Use 1 as the centre patch. Join 2–7, then 8–19.

Sewing by machine

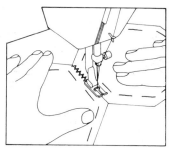

When the patches have been backed with paper and tacked in the usual way place them edge to edge right side up and machine stitch over them.

Streak of lightning

A contemporary quilt using a simple, traditional pattern with vivid effect. This pattern is also known as *Brickwall* or *Steps*.

Materials Use woollen or heavy-weight cottons with maximum colour contrast.

Uses This pattern with its bold rectangles, makes it suitable for a beginner's quilt – cot size or larger.

Construction This patchwork quilt is similar in construction to the one opposite, and is the easiest pattern to make using a machine. Sew the rectangles into rows, then join the rows, keeping the seams as straight as possible. Add a separate binding around the edge.

Repeat pattern

Join the rectangles into horizontal rows, then join the rows together.

Reds on the bed

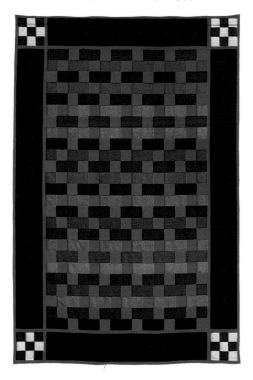

A contemporary utility quilt, made from tailors' samples of suiting fabrics. Bold quilting around the borders complements the simple design; the corners are filled with nine-patch blocks.

Materials Suiting fabrics in stripes and checks are used. The quilt is lined with a blanket for extra warmth.

Uses This basic pattern is suitable for a beginner's quilt.

Construction A machine is best for sewing these heavier fabrics. First the patches are pieced into rows then the rows are sewn together. The borders are added last and the three layers are quilted and tufted together.

| **Repeat pattern** | **Nine-patch** |

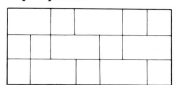

I	2	3
4	5	6
7	8	9

Sew the squares and rectangles into rows, then join them together.

Sew 1–3, 4–6, and 7–9. Join rows to make one block.

PIECED BLOCKS

A pieced block is usually a square made up from individual shapes. Such patterns developed out of necessity from poorer times when people lived in extremely cramped conditions where working on a full-size quilt would have been impossible. This method employed scraps of fabric which were skilfully re-used for making warm bedcovers. The blocks were sewn individually and then assembled. The repeated block pattern is very typical of traditional American patchwork.

Log cabin

Pennsylvanian quilt 1860-70 The most famous of all patchwork patterns, *Log cabin* blocks can be arranged to give a variety of patterns. This one, called *Barn raising*, represents the laid-out segments of a barn section before erection. Traditionally the central red patch represents the hearth and the light and dark sides represent the firelight and shadows.

Materials This pattern depends on definite light and dark shades and most types of fabric are suitable including both plain and patterned materials.

Uses Four blocks make a simple, attractive cushion but more variety of pattern can be achieved on a larger project.

Construction The *Log cabin* is one of the few patterns that does not need templates. The fabrics are cut into strips and sewn around a central square to form a larger square. The pattern can be sewn by hand or easily pieced by machine. The position of the red and green strips has been alternated in each block to give a more varied pattern.

Log cabin block

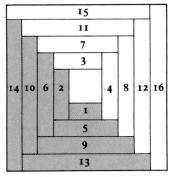

Log cabin *patterns can have any number of strips. The strips are stitched on in the order shown.*

Evening star

English quilt 1820-30 A beautiful Georgian quilt made from a rich selection of printed fabrics. Lower right block shows the traditional "deliberate" mistake, made to avoid competition with God's own perfection.

Materials This quilt combines a selection of richly-patterned fabrics, perhaps from a sample book.

Uses A good beginner's block, it can be used as a single block or an all-over pattern.

Construction This is a simple star block that can be made easily with a machine or by hand.

Evening star block

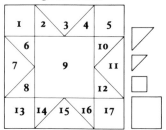

Join the pieces onto 3 separate rows. Sew 1–5, 6–12 and 13–17. Piece the rows into one block.

In this quilt, pieced blocks have been alternated with plain blocks – a simple way of increasing the quilt size.

Adding plain blocks

The blocks have been pieced together diagonally so extra quarter- and half-plain blocks have been made to complete the straight edges. Join the blocks into rows, then sew the rows together.

Odeon

A contemporary wall-hanging using bold, colourful geometric shapes built up to give a strong visual impact. It evolved from scraps and shapes left over from cutting previous quilts. Made from polyester cottons, it is machine pieced and hand quilted.

Rainbow squares

A contemporary quilt, using a colourful strip design.

Materials Closely-woven cotton or woollen fabrics are best.
Uses The bright colours make this pattern most effective repeated on a quilt or wall-hanging. The quilt only needs a few blocks and can be quickly made on a machine.

Construction Although a different colour arrangement is used, this pattern is made in the same way as the standard *Log cabin* and *Courthouse steps* block. The finished blocks are set with lattice strips and a deep border is added to increase the overall size.

One block

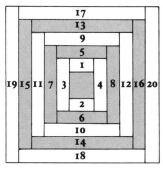

Cut the fabric into strips and join them in the order shown.

Drunkard's path

Late nineteenth-century American quilt Sometimes traditional patterns are a visual representation of an idea; this simple two-patch block is a twisting, difficult-to-negotiate path for the inebriated.

Materials Closely-woven cotton is most suitable for piecing curves.
Uses As an all-over repeat or as a single block for a cushion top.

Construction The easiest way to assemble this pattern for a repeat is to make a number of sixteen-patch blocks and to sew them by hand without papers.

Sixteen-patch block

Each 16-patch block should contain 8 patches with the dark as the larger piece and 8 with the dark as the smaller piece. Set them together making four rows of 4, 2-patch blocks.
Curves are more difficult to sew. First pin in the corners matching pencil lines, then pin in the centre and pin again until the fabric is eased into place.

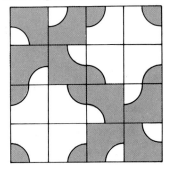

Double Irish chain

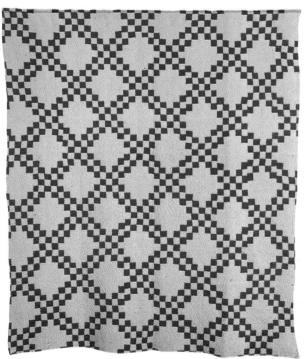

Late nineteenth-century American quilt A two-block pattern which is easy to make, although complex in appearance.

Materials Plain or small-patterned cotton fabrics are best.
Uses It is most suitable for an all-over repeat pattern.

Construction It is much easier to plan this design on graph paper because it can be a confusing pattern to piece. The pattern is a five-patch block alternated with a plain block which has a small square appliquéd onto each corner. Traditionally the plain blocks are quilted following the square patterns on the pieced blocks.

Sew 1–5, 6–10, 11–15, 16–20, 21–25. Join rows into a block. For the second block take a plain square the same size and appliqué a square onto each corner. Alternate the plain and pieced blocks to give a chain pattern.

Five-patch block   **Appliqué block**

1	2	3	4	5
6	7	8	9	10
11	12	13	14	15
16	17	18	19	20
21	22	23	24	25

Prairie queen

American utility quilt 1910 A typical nine-patch pattern, made from shirting fabrics. The darker lattice gives a window-pane effect.

Materials The blocks can be made from a scrap-bag but extra fabric is needed for the lattice strips.

Uses A pattern that can be coloured to give endless variations, it is suitable for large or small projects.

Construction This is a very easy block to assemble and can be pieced on the machine. Add the lattice strips separately.

Prairie queen block

Start with the top row and make up the three separate squares. Join 1 and 2, 3–10, 11 and 12. Join the three squares together. Continue in this way making up the second and third rows. Join the rows together, carefully matching the seams.

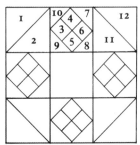

Adding lattice strips Two templates are needed for the lattice strips: a rectangular template as long as the side of the block being set, and a square template to make up the width of the lattice strip. In this case the square is the same four-patch used in the main block.

The lattice strips are pieced in the same way as a single block. Alternate rows of blocks and strips of lattice with rows of lattice with square intersections.

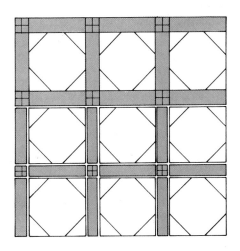

Kathryn wheel

A modern quilt in which the symmetrical pattern creates an illusion of curved lines. The shapes are accentuated with bright, contrasting colours.

Materials Use plain and printed closely-woven cotton fabrics.
Uses This pattern is suitable for a larger project such as wall-hanging or quilt.

Construction Although this pattern looks complicated it is easy to piece once the colour arrangement has been planned. To make a draft pattern, first trace the top left-hand quarter and then rotate it clockwise, a quarter each time to make the remaining three sections. Colour it several ways to make different patterns.
Once you have chosen the colours, complete the design by working in quarters. Sew two quarters together then sew the halves into one piece. Add a separate border.

One quarter of the pattern

*Each quarter of the
pattern is made up
from five rows. Join
1–12, 13–24, 25–36,
37–49 and 50–60.
Then join the rows
together. Repeat the
section three more
times, then join
together.*

1		4	7	10	11
2	3		5 6 8	9	12
14	15		17	21	24
13		16	19 18 20	22	23
27		30	31	34	35
26 28	25 29		32	33	36
37	41		44	45	47
38 40					48
39	42	43	46	49
50	53	54	58	59
51	52	55	56 57	60

City nights

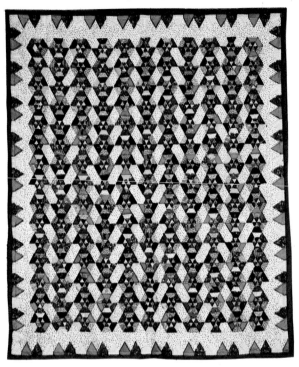

A modern quilt using larger-pieced hexagons set with triangles which form diamonds. It is similar to the traditional *Spider's web* block.

Materials Cotton fabrics with varying small prints are used to give a textured effect. Heavier fabrics such as corduroys and tweeds could be used for larger-size blocks.

Uses This pattern is particularly suitable for a large project where it can be repeated.

Construction Although the pattern is made from blocks, it is actually pieced together in horizontal strips. Three separate templates are needed – all constructed from a hexagon. The pattern evolves by rotating the composite triangle six times and by the counterchange of light and dark fabrics.

Borders For the border, the triangles used in the main pattern are repeated around the edge in contrasting colours, followed by an outer strip of matching rectangles.

To frame the design, the backing fabric has been folded over to the front to make a self-binding.

One block

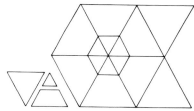

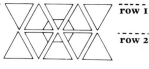

row 1

row 2

This pattern is easier to put together in rows.

Border

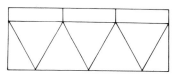

A two-patch design makes a contrasting sharp-edged border to this pattern.

Weather vane

American quilt 1890 Weather vanes were commonplace on barn roofs in nineteenth-century America. This bold utility quilt is made from remnants of check shirts, held together by a lattice pattern.

Materials Use scraps of fabric of similar weights.
Uses This pattern is suited to cushions or quilts.

Construction Sometimes when sewing pieced blocks it is easier to divide the large pieces into smaller units to avoid sewing into corners. Dotted lines suggest additional seams.

Weather-vane block

Sew 1-3, then 4 and 5. Join together. Sew 6-8 then 9 and 10. Join together. Join these two small blocks together, then add 11. Make up the remaining three-quarters of the block in the same way. Join the quarters into halves ; piece together.

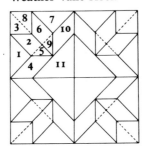

Lattice construction Use lattice strips with blocks which are quite different in colour. When setting blocks together with lattices on the diagonal, additional quarter- and half-size blocks are needed. The construction is the same as for a single block; join the pieces together in rows then join the rows together.

Start piecing at the top left corner. Join 1st and 2nd rows together. Sew together the individual pieces in the 3rd row, and add to the first 2. Continue in this way until the top is completed. The quarter- and half-size blocks are used to "square up" the edges of the finished top.

Harvest sun

American quilt 1880 This pattern is known as *Harvest sun* in the Midwest and *Ship's wheel* in Massachusetts. The block is made from an eight-pointed star, radiating outwards to form a linked pattern.

Materials This pattern is easier to make up using closely-woven cottons. The large areas of white fabric give a feeling of lightness to the quilt.

Uses A pattern with a variety of uses, it can be set to give a repeat pattern, as seen on this quilt, or used individually for cushions or small projects.

Construction The making up of this pattern is similar to the *Sunburst* construction p.24. The block is based on an eight-pointed star set diagonally. The segments are made individually then joined: first into twos, then fours. Finally the halves are joined along the centre seam making a complete star pattern. It is important to match the eight points in the centre.

Template and one segment

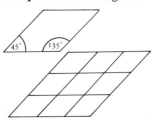

Each segment is made from nine long diamonds 45°-135°.

Finishing Set each star into a square by adding extra squares and right angles. Then set each block diagonally to make a linking pattern. Add plain strip borders.

Setting blocks diagonally

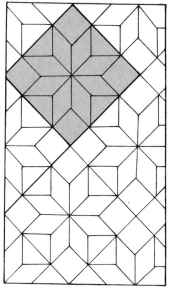

When setting the blocks diagonally, additional quarter- and half-pieced blocks are needed to fill in the edges.

Birds in the air

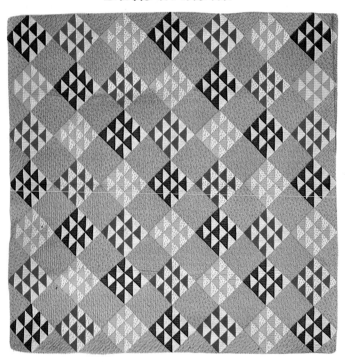

Mennonite quilt 1870 Many of the traditional patchwork blocks were based on abstract patterns taken from everyday life. This is one of the oldest blocks and is evocative of birds in flight.

Materials Because of its small-sized triangles this pattern was often used for a scrap quilt. A limited colour range as shown gives a more formal design. Use closely-woven cottons.
Uses This pattern is mainly used, and is most suitable, for an all-over, edge-to-edge repeat.

Construction Repeat blocks can easily be sewn on a machine. These are set diagonally and alternated with plain squares. The block is a nine patch.

Join 1-2, 3-4, and 5-6. Join into one row. Continue in this way for the next two rows. Join the three rows together, making one block.

Birds-in-the-air block

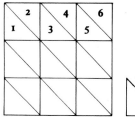

Nine patch

American quilt 1870 A simple utility quilt made from a basic nine-patch block. Blue was the earliest fast dye and a popular colour for patchwork quilts.

Materials Closely-woven cotton with a small pattern.
Uses The scale of the block is best suited to a quilt.

Construction The pieced blocks are alternated with plain squares and set diagonally. Simple strip borders are added separately.

Nine-patch block

There are several ways of piecing this block. The simplest is to sew it into three horizontal rows. Join 1-8, 9-17, 18-25. Join the rows together into one block.

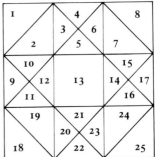

Double pyramids

An American quilt using a very old pattern from Virginia. The generous area of white appears to open up the design.

Materials Plain or small-patterned closely-woven fabrics are ideal.
Uses Can be used in single blocks or set edge-to-edge to create a more compact pattern.

Construction These blocks are set diagonally and joined with lattice strips to create an open pattern.

It is best to piece all the composite triangles first before making the complete block.
Join the larger pieces into rows and then into one block.

Double pyramid block

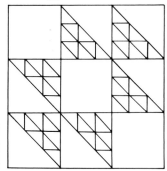

Balloons

A contemporary cot quilt in a symmetrical nine-patch design which creates the illusion of curved lines. When these blocks are repeated unexpected patterns develop.

Materials The best choice is closely-woven cotton in appropriate patterns and colours.
Uses This is an interesting block with endless colour variations, each creating a new design. It is most suitable for quilts or wall-hangings but is not a beginner's pattern.

Construction It is not always necessary to repeat whole blocks when designing a patchwork pattern. This quilt uses half-blocks on the top, left and bottom edge to create a more interesting asymmetrical

design. It is essential to make a scaled drawing of more complex designs beforehand, so that it is available for reference when putting the pattern together. This design can be edge-to-edge or have a separate border added and can be sewn by hand or machine.

Arrangement of blocks

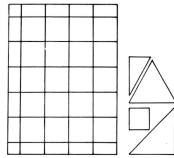

Four half-blocks are added to the top and bottom rows, and 5 half-blocks to the left edge. Quarter-blocks are used for the two corners.

One block

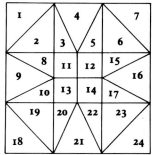

Join 1–2, and 3–5, and 6–7. Join 8–10, and 11–14 and 15–17. Join 18–19, and 20–22, and 23–24. Join the three rows together.

Burgoyne surrounded

American quilt 1850-60 Quilt patterns often had names of political significance, such as *Lincoln's platform* or *Free trade*. *Burgoyne surrounded* refers to an incident from the Revolutionary period. These patterns served as visual representations of such events or ideas. In this pattern the larger red English infantry square is encircled by files of small squares, the American irregulars.

Materials The military connection with the pattern and small size of squares suggests red and white closely-woven cotton, though it would also make an interesting pattern reversed out of a dark background.

Uses When considering use, it should be remembered that this is one of the larger block patterns. It is unsuitable for smaller projects if used as a repeat pattern.

Construction The fact that individual blocks are pieced with lattice strips is not apparent at first. The basic fifteen-patch block pattern is extended by nine-patch blocks within the lattice strips. It is advisable to piece the blocks then add the lattice strips separately.

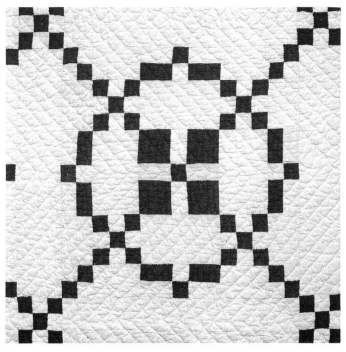

Repeated block with lattice strips

The main blocks are easier to work if the individual patches are made into bigger units, as suggested by the dotted lines. The repeat block shows how the pattern is extended by the nine patch in the lattice strips.

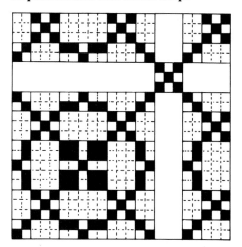

Patterned bars

A modern quilt using traditional pieced blocks in an unusual design. This quilt has been sewn by hand using papers but it can be made very easily by machine, with a variety of plain and printed cotton fabrics.

Pieced blocks used above. Top to bottom.

1 **Nine patch**
2 **Variable star**
3 **Ribbons**
4 **Tumbling blocks**
5 **World without end**
6 **Broken dishes**
7 **Pieced star**
8 **Diamond star**

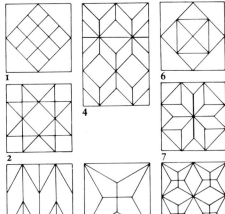

Houses

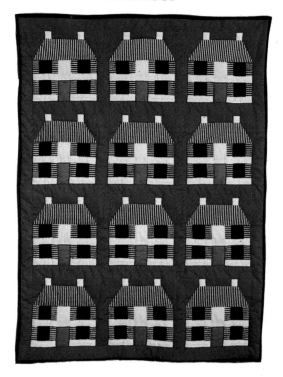

A contemporary English quilt which uses the basic house shape in an uncomplicated design. This is reminiscent of the traditional *Schoolhouse* block.

Materials Use plain and geometric-patterned cottons.
Uses It can be used as a single image or repeated for a child's quilt.

Construction An example of a visual image that has been simplified into straight lines for easy piecing. The blocks are joined with lattice strips.

House block

The dotted lines suggest additional seams for easier piecing. Sew the smaller units together into the five rows then join the rows making one block.

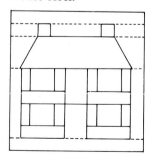

Vampire butterflies

American quilt 1930's An unusual figurative patchwork quilt featuring evil-looking butterflies with stings in their tails.

Materials This pattern can be best made from a variety of plain and printed closely-woven cottons.
Uses The butterfly motif is a decorative pattern that can be used singly for cushions and clothes, or as a repeat all-over pattern for a quilt. It could also be combined with floral blocks.

Construction For piecing figurative work it is better to simplify the image into individual geometric pieces which can be easily sewn together with straight lines by hand or machine. These blocks have been set diagonally using half- and quarter-blocks to fill out the edges. Stitch the butterfly details separately.

Assemble the block in two main pieces. For the first piece sew the patches in three separate stages.
a. Join 1 and 2
b. Join 3, 4, 5, 6, 7 and 8
c. Join 9, 10, 11 and 12
Next, join the last two groups together then add to 1 and 2.

For the second main piece, join in two stages.
a. Join 13, 14, 15, 16, 17 and 18
b. Join 19, 20, 21 and 22
Again, join these two groups together.
Sew the two main pieces together, making one block.

Butterfly block

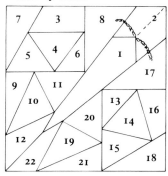

FRAMED OR MEDALLION

Framed designs are a complete contrast to the all-over patterns made from pieced blocks. The characteristic of this design is a planned centre-piece surrounded by a series of frames or borders. It can be made with patchwork or appliqué. In the early nineteenth century, special panels were printed and used in the centre of quilts. Medallion patterns were typical of early English patchworks.

English medallion

An early nineteenth-century patchwork coverlet showing a great variety of fabrics. Patchwork was very popular in England at that time and showed great skill and economy in the use of fabrics, which were often difficult to obtain. These utility patchworks were very different to the extravagant coverlets of the latter part of the century which lacked the earlier spontaneity of design.

Materials This patchwork shows, above all else, the thrifty and ingenious use of fabric scraps.
Uses Framed or medallion patterns are only suitable for quilts or large wall-hangings.

Construction This design, built around a centre pattern, uses a basic four-patch block divided into triangles, alternated with printed cotton strips and zigzag pieced borders.
This coverlet is shaped to fit a four poster bed.

Four-patch block	**Zigzag border**	**Sewing triangles**

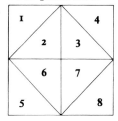

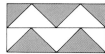

A zigzag border is made from two rows of pieced triangles.

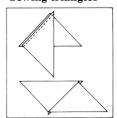

A simple block to piece. Join the patches into two rows, 1-4 and 5-8. Join the rows.

When sewing the triangles match the seam lines not the cutting lines.

Peacock

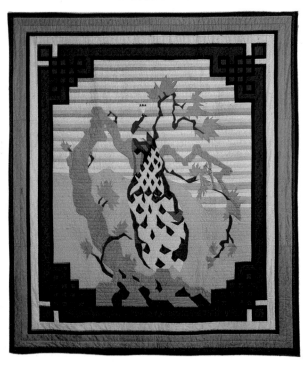

A contemporary quilt following the framed tradition in patch-work, but adapting a border from a Chinese lattice design, to complement the formalized styling of the tree and peacock.

Materials Hand-dyed fabrics. See p.90.

Construction This quilt is distinguished by its imaginative piecing. Each pictorial image is broken down into small pieces which are then joined together into strips. The border can be made from a repeated block but for the individual images, such as the peacock and tree, a full-size drawing has to be made from which the templates are cut.

The quilt is machine pieced and quilted with a sink stitch (the stitches are hidden in the seam).

Lattice border

Dotted lines indicate additional seams for piecing a lattice border.

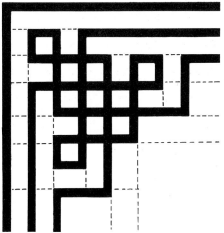

Amish medallion

An Amish quilt, Iowa 1935 The Amish, like the Mennonites, shared a preference for a plain simple lifestyle. Their quilts, however, display powerful geometric designs using intense solid colours.

Materials Plain closely-woven cottons or woollen fabrics.
Uses As a quilt or wall-hanging.

Construction A series of borders surrounding a central star. Each border is finely stitched in a different quilting pattern. Follow the same sequence for attaching borders as shown opposite.

Medallion pattern

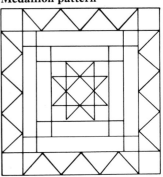

Square within a square

English wedding quilt 1870 A quilt using a basic four-patch block.

Materials Contrasting plain and printed cotton fabrics are ideal.
Uses Large-size quilts.

Construction This pattern has been worked out on a square grid
beforehand so that each piece fits perfectly. Piece the blocks into the
required lengths before assembling a medallion pattern.

*When piecing a
medallion pattern
always work from the
centre outwards.
Join 1 and 2 to the
centre design, then
add 3 and 4.
Continue in this way
of adding top and
bottom strips then
side pieces, following
the sequence on the
diagram.*

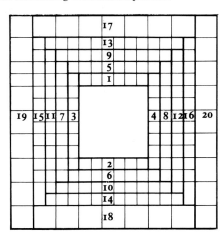

CRAZY

Crazy patchwork first evolved out of necessity and enabled even the tiniest scraps to be used to create warm bedcovers. However, during the second half of the nineteenth century, crazy patchwork became extremely ornate. Rich brocades and silks were used and overstitched with a great variety of embroidery patterns.
Crazy patchwork patterns were later also used for cushions, mats and curtains and became associated with Victorian eclecticism.

Late nineteenth-century English crazy patchwork throw
Crazy quilts were no longer used as bedcovers but were draped over sofas (throws) and used purely for decoration.

Crazy squares

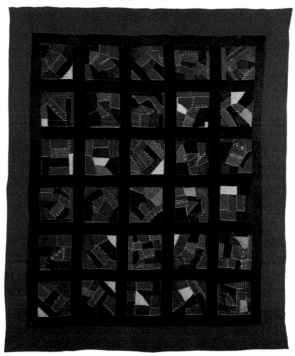

A Mennonite quilt A typical example of Mennonite work displaying their distinctive use of bold colours to create a utility quilt.

Materials Most fabrics are suitable for crazy patterns and it is a good way of using up scraps.
Uses Crazy patchwork is very adaptable and can be used for clothes as well as cushions, quilts and even curtains and tablecloths.

Construction No templates are needed for crazy patchwork. Overlapping scraps are sewn onto a foundation fabric. Crazy patchwork can be assembled in a large, single piece or as individual blocks which are joined.

Begin in one corner, pin first piece in position. Take second piece, fold under raw edge and tack in position. Continue overlapping and tacking in position until the foundation fabric is covered. Hemstitch around the edges.

Crazy block

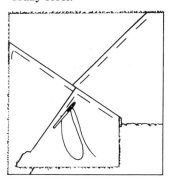

APPLIQUE

Appliqué means applying one fabric to another. Most of the early patterns were flower and bird motifs cut from partly-worn fabrics, often Indian chintzes, and stitched to a new foundation. This technique was known as "Broderie Perse" and developed when textiles were scarce and expensive. Appliqué patterns can be divided into two categories: freely drawn and cut images, often showing figurative work, and symmetrical patterns.

Flower basket

Pennsylvanian Dutch quilt 1920 A lively and spontaneous design combining appliqué and patchwork. The Pennsylvania Dutch patterns were quite distinctive, using many motifs such as hearts and flowers derived from their use of traditional folk art decoration and strong colour.

Materials Use a variety of plain and printed closely-woven cotton fabrics.

Uses The spontaneity of this technique makes it very suitable for children's projects.

Construction This technique is often referred to as "Scissor painting". The shapes have been cut freely and directly from the fabric. The patchwork basket was sewn onto the centre square then the borders were added in a similar way to a medallion quilt. The stems, leaves and flowers were added last.

Egyptian appliqué

Enormous appliquéd tent wall-hangings were made in Egypt with visually striking geometric patterns often Islamic-inspired, and having an Arabic inscription. Appliqué was often heraldic in nature and special patterns were associated with a particular family. The appliqué was cut from paper or muslin templates and tacked onto the coloured cloth. The cloth was cut to shape then appliquéd onto the background fabric, with a hemstitch. The stitching was often crude but these designs were vital, and skilfully assembled to create a spontaneous lively pattern. The technique of appliqué is quite well established throughout the African continent and is used for commercial banners and flags as well as clothes.

Hawaiian appliqué

A contemporary quilt showing the distinctive formalized design of Hawaiian appliqué. The patterns are made from whole cloth and usually show only two colours. The quilts are thickly padded and outlined with narrow rows of quilting.

Materials Two different-coloured squares of cotton fabric; the background square must be slightly larger.
Uses Single patterns can be used for cushions, larger or repeated patterns for quilts.

Construction Carefully press the two squares, folding both in the same direction; first in half, then into quarters and finally into eights. Choose a traditional design or make your own. Pin the design on the top layer of the folded appliqué fabric and trace off. Cut out the design. Carefully unfold design onto right side of base fabric, matching the diagonal folds. Pin into position, then tack the appliqué. Start sewing in the centre of the design, roll edges under approximately 3mm ($\frac{1}{8}$in). (Do this with the needle.) Working clockwise sew with a neat overcast stitch, preferably using quilting thread in the same colour as the applied fabric.

Cutting the fabric

Trace the design and pin through the eight layers before cutting.

71

Wild flower wreaths

A modern quilt that is an unusual variation on the traditional wreath motif. The pattern is normally variable with different flowers, but this quilt has unusual combinations of thistles, honeysuckle and dandelions.

Materials Choose a variety of plain and printed cottons of equal weights and fine textures that will not fray.
Uses The wreath motif can be used singly or combined in a quilt.

Construction When small-size pieces are used, wreath patterns are best sewn by hand. Assemble the individual units first, turning under the edges and tacking. Press the foundation square diagonally to give the centre. Draw on a large circle the size of the desired wreath. Cut a bias strip for the wreath, 20mm (¾in) wide, turn under edges on each side. Place bias strip around the circle and tack the inside edge first. Pull the outer edge until it lies flat on the background, tack. Place, pin and tack the individual motifs around the circle. Then finally stitch in position, using a hem stitch or decorative cross stitch. Add extra details such as twining stems with embroidery stitches.

Finishing The wreaths are appliquéd on individual blocks which are then pieced with patchwork shapes and framed with appliquéd borders. The swag borders are cut from folded fabric. The construction of the quilt is similar to that of the framed medallion patterns, starting at the centre and working outwards.

Turkey track block

Prepare all the shapes, then place 1 on the background square, matching the centre points and diagonals. Pin in position. Add the four centre shapes (2s), pin and tack. Then add the 3s, pin and tack. Finally sew down with a small neat hem stitch. Dotted lines indicate the edges tucked under.

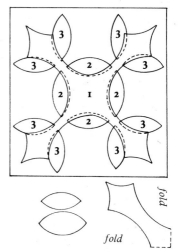

Oriental vases

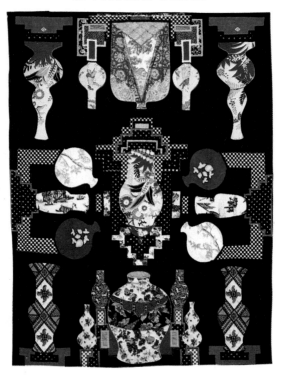

A modern wall-hanging based on the formal arrangements of stylized oriental vases. A dramatic and imaginative use of patterned fabrics where the different scales of pattern are skilfully contrasted to suit the appropriate shapes.

Materials This pattern provides the opportunity of using a selection of exotic fabrics.

Uses These stylized shapes can be used individually or grouped into formal patterns for larger projects.

Construction This wall-hanging illustrates a different appliqué technique – couching. The edges of appliquéd motifs are left raw and covered with cord, ribbon or bias binding. It is a particularly effective way of decorating the edges and gives a variety of effects. The shape of the motif can be emphasized by using a light cord, as shown on the large foreground vase opposite.

When planning a design like this, a full-scale drawing of the shapes should be made first. These can then be cut out and arranged to make the pattern and also used as templates for cutting out the fabric. A firm background fabric is needed on which to sew the individual shapes. Build up the design in layers, starting with the underlying shapes first. To make the fabrics opaque, which is

necessary when overlapping shapes, use the finest iron-on inter-facing. This also keeps the fabrics firm and prevents fraying.

Couching Machine sewing can be used for wider couching materials such as bias binding but when applying thin cords it is easier to sew by hand.

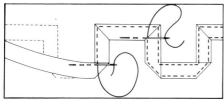

Make sure that neither the braid nor ground fabric puckers and that the curves are neatly turned by folding the braid over.

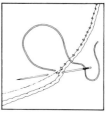

Secure the laid cord at regular intervals with couching stitches. Finish by taking threads to the back.

Kaleidoscope

A modern quilt using a pattern of unusual appliqué motifs.

Materials An arrangement of bright primary colours on a white ground creates a sparkling design.
Uses Can be used as individual motifs or grouped together to form a more elaborate design.

Construction This pattern is made up of identical quarters, each based on a grid of thirty-six squares. Each square is appliquéd separately then joined together with plain ones to make up the size. A separate border is added.

One quarter of pattern

First appliqué the squares then make them up into a six by six larger square, following the diagram. If any pieces of your pattern take up more than one square, add these after the smaller squares have been joined.

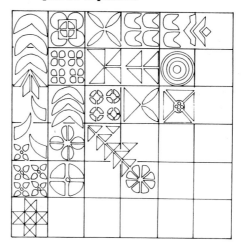

81

Pine tree

American New England quilt 1880 The pine tree was a favourite symbol in New England and used on coins and flags. Quilts from that area were noted for their graphic pictorial patterns. This pattern combines appliqué and patchwork and the blocks are contained within a saw-tooth border.

Materials Closely-woven cotton is most suitable for the small patchwork pieces.
Uses Set edge-to-edge or use as a single unit.

Construction Each pine tree block is basically a nine patch. The blocks are set diagonally and alternated with plain squares. Sew by hand or machine.

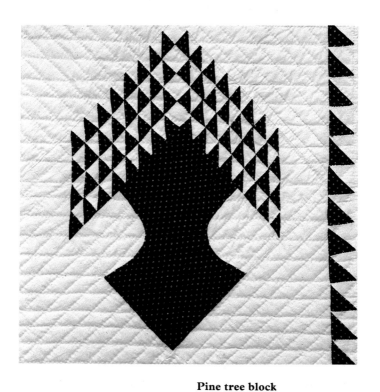

Make up the six individual patchwork squares – note that the corner pieced block has a different pattern. Turn under the curved edges of the appliqué shape, the straight raw edges will be hidden in the seams. Then join the squares together. Join 1 and 2, then sew to the larger appliquéd square 3. Join 4, 5, 6 in a strip and join to the main piece.

Pine tree block

Dyed and Sprayed

In the last few years designers have been experimenting with new techniques in the design and construction of patchworks. Many traditional patterns are still made but the craft has been extended to include new materials, dyes and equipment. Today's designers are more interested in making individual projects using fabrics coloured by air-brushing and controlled dyeing which often have greater textural interest produced by pleating and machine quilting.

Blue forest

A modern quilt with a tall pine tree pattern which creates interesting shades of lights and darks.

Materials A selection of plain and striped fabrics that have been dyed together in one colour. Pure cotton is more receptive to dyes and the colour is much deeper than cotton polyester mixtures.

Uses Suitable for cushions and wall-hangings; the dyeing technique is useful in coordinating odd fabric batches.

Construction The fabric is dyed beforehand in a single colour bath; the different materials still retain individual tonal values which create a watercolour effect. Use a reliable commercial hot or cold dye. Iron the materials before use.

To recreate the pattern, use large pieces that can be sewn quickly on a machine. Join the patches into rows, then sew into one piece. Add a separate border.

Repeat pattern

Two templates are needed for this pattern. Piece all the large rectangles first then alternate with the small ones and make into rows.

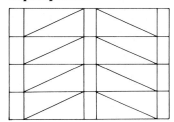

Diamonds

A contemporary quilt with a bold geometric pattern showing a dramatic contrast of scale. The larger pieces are sewn together but the horizontal strips of diamonds have been sprayed with an airbrush.

Materials Plain cotton fabric (the same weight as the other fabrics in the pattern), airbrush, fabric ink, masking film.
Uses For any large-scale project or when additional patterned fabric is required for a particular design, especially when a small patterned area is desired.

Construction This is a simple pattern and should be made on a machine. It is assembled in three main sections: the central strip, and the two flanking strips. The two side strips are basically repeat patterns alternating pieced and printed strips. For the printed strips an airbrush has been used to reproduce a pattern on the fabric that suits the rest of the patchwork. It is a quicker alternative to sewing the shapes which would take much longer and be too exacting.

Fabric dyes are used: these are made permanent by pressing with a hot iron on the wrong side of the sprayed fabric. A stencil or mask is cut, from card or special adhesive film, for each colour and shape and the lightest colour sprayed first. It is essential to keep the fabric to be sprayed as flat as possible. When the spraying is complete trim the fabric to the correct size, machine quilt and then piece into the pattern. The middle section is made in large pieced triangles. Join all the sections together, add backing and separate bound edge. The central panel is quilted in large stitches with crochet cotton. Tufting is used to keep the three layers together in the side panels.

Tinted shadows

A contemporary wall-hanging using sprayed squares of fabric that have been tucked and pleated to create three-dimensional textures.

Materials Polyester cotton fabric, air gun and fabric dyes.
Uses Can be used for large or small soft furnishing projects.

Construction First wash the fabric then fold, pleat and tuck the individual squares; hold the tucks down with machine stitches. Spray on the colour, grading it from light to dark. Press with a hot iron to make the colour permanent.
Join all the squares together. Add a separate lining and border.

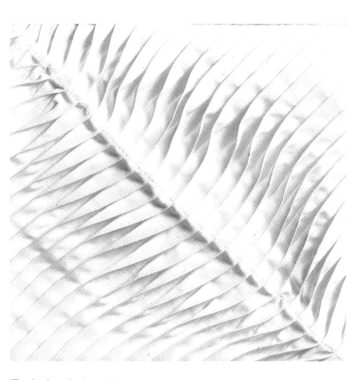

Tucked and pleated patterns

89

Flying ducks

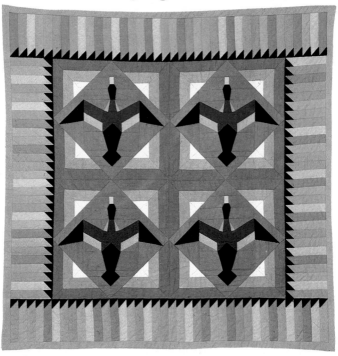

A contemporary wall-hanging with an imaginative pictorial pattern which uses a repeated block surrounded by strip borders. The images are enhanced by the variety of colours used, and skilfully simplified for machine piecing.

Materials Plain closely-woven cotton fabric, fibre reactive (cold water) dyes.
Uses Both small- and large-scale projects and where it is necessary to have complete control over the colours used in the patchwork.

Construction Make a draft colour pattern and dye the fabric to match. Wash fabric first, dye by hand or washing machine, and then rinse and boil with a detergent to remove excess dye. Join small units into bigger pieces. On the duck block, the main body is assembled first, then the head, wings and tail are added, making a square shape. This square is set diagonally and extra triangles added to each corner to make another square. Four duck blocks are then joined to make a larger square. The borders are pieced and sewn into strips. The strips are added on both sides then longer ones for the top and bottom. The complete pieced top is then quilted by machine using a sink stitch (running it along the seam so that it is hidden) and a separate binding added.

Duck block

Join all the individual pieces to make up the main units 1–17. Join 2 and 3 to 1. Then add 4 and 5. Then 6–9, working clockwise. This completes the duck image. Join 10–11, 12–13, 14–15 and 16–17. Add one of these triangles to each side of the duck image, thus setting it diagonally into a square. Make up 3 more squares and join together.

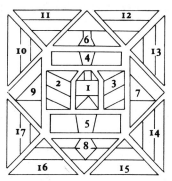

Strip border

Join the 2-patch strips first, then assemble into rows.

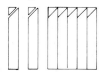

91

Sprayed quilt I

A contemporary wall-hanging that uses a sprayed and quilted geometric pattern to give varying intensities of colour built up with tiny dots.

Materials Satin acetate, disperse dyes (bleedproof), spraygun with splatter cup or toothbrush, masking film.
Uses Patterns suitable for quilts, cushion covers, curtains and clothes.

Construction To recreate this effect on any project, you apply the colour before making up. First mark out the pattern as lightly as possible on the fabric. Mask around the area to be sprayed and gradually build up the colour from tiny dots using a splatter cup.

When the spraying is complete seal the colour with steam, this can be done over a saucepan of boiling water. Finally wash the fabric in hot water and detergent to remove the excess dye. Press flat. The fabric is now ready to use. This technique can be used for large areas of fabric or smaller pieces which can then be joined together.

On this wall-hanging the geometric shapes are further emphasized with straight lines of machine quilting.

Trip to the moon

A contemporary cot quilt The design has been painted on fabric then appliquéd to the background.

Materials White cotton fabric, fabric paints or crayons.
Uses Suitable for illustrative appliqué and children's work.

Construction Draw an outline of the design onto the fabric and add the colours with a paint brush or airbrush. Always keep the fabric flat with masking tape. When the painting is dry, press several times on the wrong side with a hot iron; this makes the design permanent. Cut out and appliqué in the usual way.
The colours are washable, but care should be taken with dry cleaning.

Index

Acknowledgments

Quilts reproduced by permission of

Duttons 64
Jane Kasmin 22, 65
Joen Lask, 21 Antiques 18, 20, 26, 30, 32, 36, 37, 38, 48, 50, 51, 54, 66, 74, 76, 82
Private collection 44, 46
Ron Simpson and Paul Taylor 24, 58, 60, 67, 68
Strawberry Fayre 70
The American Museum in Britain, Bath 71

Quilts made by

Deirdre Amsden 28, 34, 57, 94
Margaret Brandebourg 42
Pauline Burbidge 62, 90
Mary Fogg 21
Diana Harrison 92
Iona Heath 29
Frances Anne Kemble 40 (original design by Beth and Jeffrey Gutcheon)
Christine McKechnie 56, 72
Susan Murdoch 78
Pat Novy 84
Eng Tow 88
Michele Walker 52 (original block designed by Beth and Jeffrey Gutcheon), 86
Kathern Wright Parker 35, 80

Fabrics

Liberty & Co Ltd, Strawberry Fayre

Artists

John Hutchinson
Gary Marsh

Photographers

Ian O'Leary
Steve Oliver
Andrew De Lory

Typesetting

Contact Graphics Ltd

Reproduction

F E Burman Ltd